"Hard work is great fun."

—Fred Astaire

FOOTWORK

The Story of Fred and Adele Astaire

ROXANE ORGILL

ILLUSTRATED BY

STÉPHANE JORISCH

CANDLEWICK PRESS
CAMBRIDGE, MASSACHUSETTS

One day, while Fred Astaire was waiting for his sister, Adele, to finish dancing class, he saw a pair of ballet shoes in the corner. He put them on and walked on his toes. He was four and a half.

Soon there was talk around the house about "dancing school" and "New York" and "opportunity." The talk concerned mostly Adele, but Fred was in it, too. "Adele is a born dancer," Father said, "and Fred might not be too bad."

Suitcases were packed, and one morning in 1905, Father drove Fred, Adele, and Mother in the horse-drawn buggy to the train depot. Suddenly Father was waving good-bye from the platform, and Fred was boarding the hissing, waiting train with his mother and sister. Father was to stay home in Omaha to work for the brewery and would join them from time to time. The others were traveling all the way to New York City so that Adele could go to a dancing school that Father had seen advertised in a newspaper. Adele was seven and the dancer in the family. Fred was five and along for the ride.

Fred was thrilled to ride for two days and two nights in the Pullman car. He slept with Adele in the upper berth and peeked under the window shade to watch the country roll by.

In New York, Fred followed Adele up the narrow, dark stairs to the fourth floor of the Grand Opera House. He had lessons at the Claude Alvienne dancing school, too. He liked the stick that white-haired Mr. Alvienne tapped against a wooden chair to keep time. *Tap. Tap. Tap. Tap.*

After only about a year, Mr. Alvienne wanted to put Adele and Fred in a show. He dressed them up as a bride and groom, and they tap-danced on top of a pair of wooden wedding cakes built especially for them. The cakes had flashing lights, and bells that they played with their hands and feet. Then Fred changed into a lobster costume, and Adele dressed up as a champagne glass, and they played more tunes on the cakes and danced on their toes.

The Wedding Cake Act went over big in Keyport, New Jersey—so big that it landed the children a spot on the big-time vaudeville circuit. Vaudeville was a kind of variety show. In 1906, there was no radio or television, and movies with sound hadn't been invented yet, so people went to vaudeville. For a quarter, they could see marvelous, impossible things. Joe Cook juggled while standing on a high wire. A man with no arms shuffled and dealt cards and played the violin—with his feet. Eddie Foy smiled his crooked smile like a crescent moon turned on its side and sang "Garden of Roses" in a cracked, winsome voice. There were trick bicyclists, talking dogs, a wrestling pony, and pigs playing seesaw. And Sandow, the strongest man in the world. He could hold out at arm's length two bicyclists, one in each hand.

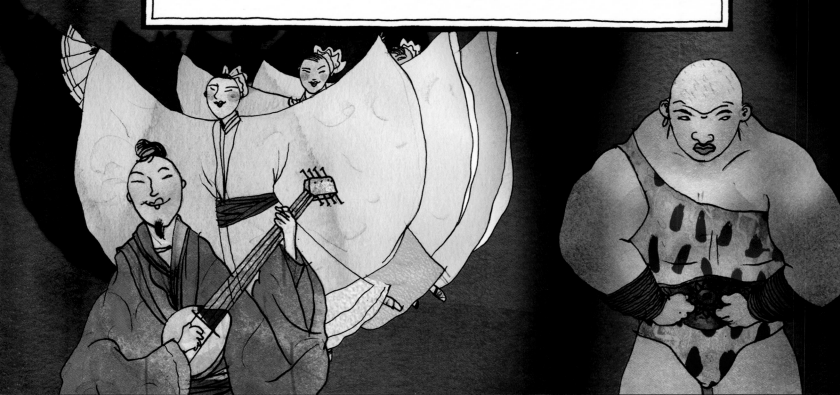

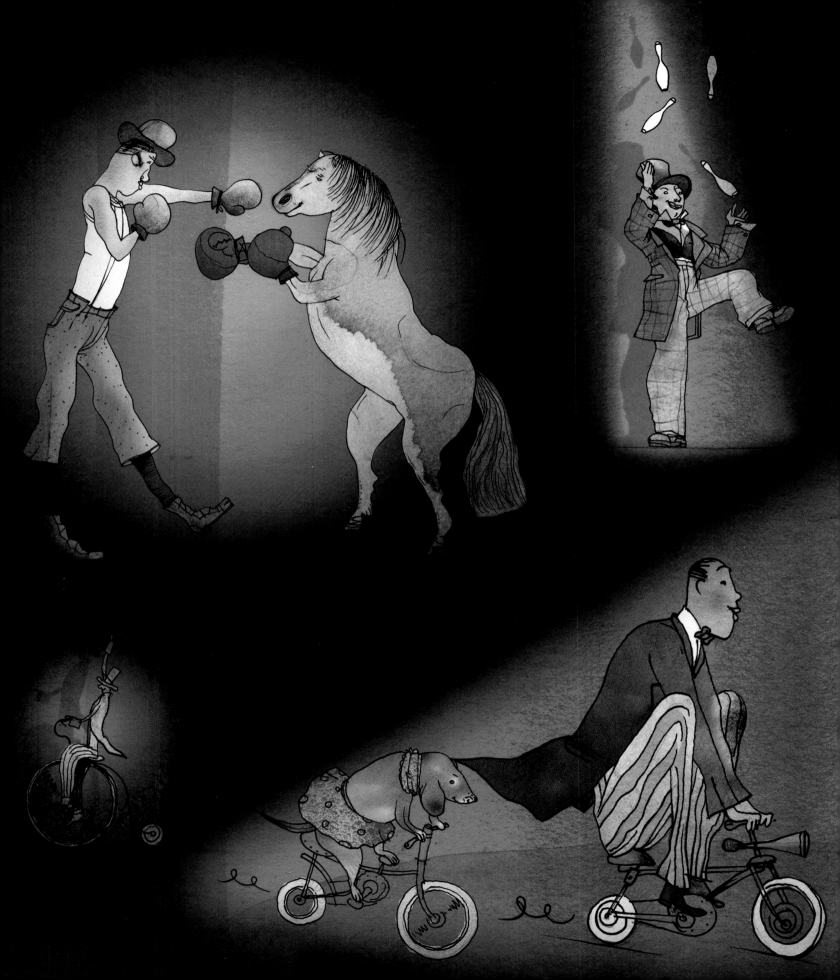

Twice a day, Fred and Adele went up onstage and did the steps Mr. Alvienne had taught them, and people clapped and cheered as if they had never seen anything like it. Afterward, Fred watched the rest of the show from the wings. He stood in the cold and spidery dark for hours and caught every wink, trick, and beat.

At the end of the week, Fred, Adele, and Mother packed up their tubes of greasepaint, their wardrobe trunks, the two wedding cakes, and a few belongings and traveled to another theater in another town.

Fred just about lived on steam trains that belched smoke and smelled of hot oil—he ate, slept, even had his lessons on the train. Mother taught the children reading, writing, and arithmetic herself, since they moved around too much to go to school. They had no friends but each other.

Lancaster, St. Paul, Newark. . . . The jumps between cities were sometimes long. Fred roamed the passenger cars and became pals with the conductor and the brakemen, who worked the track switches when the engineer wanted to add or drop a car. Adele played with her paper dolls, and Mother pasted reviews from the newspapers into a big red leather scrapbook. One read, "Two little ones, Adele and Fred, give an electrical dancing novelty in vaudeville."

Sioux City, Wilmington, Pittsburgh, and finally—back to Omaha. The whole town turned out to see Adele, now eleven, and Fred, who was nine, perform at the Orpheum Theater. The crowd stamped and shouted for more. Fred had never seen so many flowers thrown onto a stage—all for him and Adele, all because she had gone away to New York to study dancing and he had gone along for the ride, and now they had returned, top-notchers in big-time vaudeville. Fred flashed a smile, crossed one foot precisely behind the other, and took a deep bow.

Then somebody passed a huge basket of red roses across the footlights. Hiding inside was a white Pomeranian puppy. Fred knew right away whom the gift was for. Adele had been admiring the puppies in a shop window all week.

She was the one people remembered. "The little girl is especially excellent," said the newspaper clipping from Denver pasted in Mother's scrapbook. But it was Fred who offered little suggestions to Father on how to make the act better.

Spokane, Oakland, Salt Lake City. . . . The children grew, and the act began to slip a little. Adele was nearly twelve and looked like a young lady, while Fred was small for ten and looked like a little boy. They looked peculiar as bride and groom. Fred worried he was bringing down the act.

Father came to the rescue. Take a break, he said. Fred will grow taller, and everyone can have a rest. In 1909, Mother unpacked their suitcases in the upstairs of a house in Weehawken, New Jersey, to be near New York and the theaters. The children went to school. For the first time, Fred sat at a desk in a classroom smelling of chalk. When he heard the whistle blow on the Jersey Central, he was not on the train but in his own bed, listening from a distance. Mother invited the neighborhood children to pull molasses candy, and Fred and Adele made new friends. They went sledding down a long hill called "the Valley" almost all the way to Hoboken.

Two years passed. Fred was nearly as tall as his sister. It was time to go back to work.

They put together an all-new act for their first appearance in a top-notch New York vaudeville theater, Proctor's Fifth Avenue. But the manager put them first on the program, the worst spot to be. People came in late and made a racket as they slammed down the folding seats. *Bang, bang, bang-bang-bang.* Fred could hardly hear himself sing, *"When Uncle Joe plays a rag on his old banjo / Everybody starts a-swaying to and fro. . . ."* He broke out in a fearful sweat. He was dancing on his toes and playing piano at the same time, and nobody was paying any attention! There was only a twittering of applause. Fred and Adele ran to their dressing room and cried.

That evening, their names were no longer on the program. Their act had been canceled. It was a terrible blow.

Fred and Adele had been adorable little kids who did remarkable things; now they were twelve and nearly fourteen and strictly small potatoes, nowhere good enough for the big-time. But there was no question of giving up. Mother and Father wouldn't think of it. Vaudeville was the only life they knew as a family. And that wasn't all. Father's job at the brewery was about to end, and the family needed the money the children could provide.

Fred and Adele went on the small-time circuit and played in cheap, dirty places, anywhere they were asked, five and six times a day. Once they shared a program with a group of seals who did tricks. The Astaires had to climb a ladder to their dressing room, because the fishy-smelling seals got the only other dressing room, on the ground floor.

Finally, Father found a new teacher, Aurelia Coccia, who said that all they needed was a new act and to work very hard. Mr. Coccia gave them more grown-up dances: a waltz and a tango. He let Fred choose some of the songs. For six long months, he and Adele practiced the new songs and steps. They gave the act everything they had.

Fred played a detective. "Stop! Stop! Don't you dare to move! You're under arrest!" he shouted into the dark.

"What have I done to you?" Adele shot back.

The lights came on, and Adele and Fred scampered out singing, "Love Made Me a Wonderful Detective." Then they did an airy tap dance.

Adele was dainty and had a pixie smile. Fred was bony, and his ears were enormous, but he was the one who worked to make the act better. If the spotlight was the wrong color, he got the manager to change it. When the music was too fast, Fred asked the conductor, "Would you please take the second number a little slower?" If the floor was slippery, Fred filled a sock with powdered rosin, poked holes in the sock, and sprinkled the rosin on the floorboards to make them sticky. He had to do it when the manager wasn't looking, because the other performers didn't like gummy floors.

Fred worried about the floor. He worried about the music and the dances.

He worried so much that Adele called him Moaning Minnie. He liked to get to the theater early so he could warm up his muscles and run through the entire routine. Adele arrived just in time to slap on her greasepaint and zip into her costume before the curtain went up. Then she went out and skipped on her toes and sang in her squeaky, high, wobbly voice that made everyone laugh.

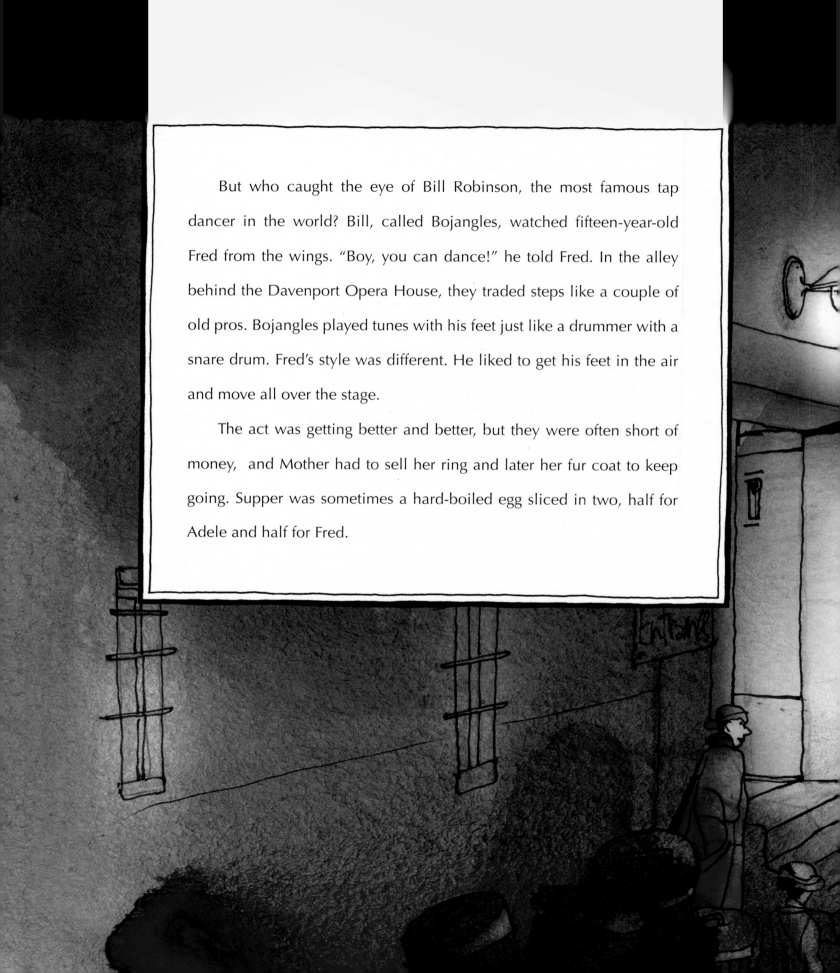

But who caught the eye of Bill Robinson, the most famous tap dancer in the world? Bill, called Bojangles, watched fifteen-year-old Fred from the wings. "Boy, you can dance!" he told Fred. In the alley behind the Davenport Opera House, they traded steps like a couple of old pros. Bojangles played tunes with his feet just like a drummer with a snare drum. Fred's style was different. He liked to get his feet in the air and move all over the stage.

The act was getting better and better, but they were often short of money, and Mother had to sell her ring and later her fur coat to keep going. Supper was sometimes a hard-boiled egg sliced in two, half for Adele and half for Fred.

Then in Chicago, the manager let Fred put rosin on the floor: "Not too much, and don't let anyone see you!" Fred and Adele, already well practiced, did their tango with no worry of a slip or a tumble, and the applause started in the balcony like a thunderclap. It rolled down through the seats and up onto the stage and nearly bowled them over. They had to take six bows. The music began for the next act, but still the audience called for them to come out and take another bow.

They had stopped the show! As showstoppers, they could work the big-time circuit again, just two shows a day, with clean dressing rooms and running water and no seals! They made top dollar, too—three hundred and fifty a week, at a time when it cost only a nickel to go to the movies.

Brooklyn, Johnstown, Baltimore, Memphis. . . . In 1917, when Fred was seventeen and Adele was almost nineteen, the Astaires were offered a chance to stop hopping from place to place and be in a musical show on Broadway in New York City. They said good-bye to vaudeville and starred in long-running musical comedies with cheery names like *Apple Blossoms* and *For Goodness' Sake.* They grew up and lived in a ritzy apartment with Mother on Park Avenue. Fred zipped around town in a Rolls-Royce.

Night after night, he and his sister sang, *"It's the whichness of the whatness and the whereness of the who / that explains most everything to us,"* and ran in a circle with their arms stuck out in front as if riding imaginary bicycles. As the orchestra played *oompah-oompah* over and over, they trotted around and around, then took a sudden turn and were gone—into the wings. The audience howled with laughter. When the Oompah Trot went right, it was a joy to do.

When it went wrong, or when anything went wrong or was just the least bit imperfect, Fred stayed late to practice. He made Adele stay, too. She wanted to go to parties with her friends, but she was fond of Fred. She called him Big Brother, even though he was younger. He was her one true friend. And so brother and sister rehearsed long into the night until every turn, tap, and tilt of the head was perfect.

Fred and Adele sailed to London in 1923, and the Prince of Wales came to see the show ten times. On another visit, Fred sang, *"Fascinatin' rhythm, you've got me on the go,"* and the prince danced along in the back of his box.

The Astaires were a knockout in London. Their pictures rolled through the streets on the sides of double-decker buses. Fred bought diamond and ruby buttons for his waistcoat. Adele bought green kid slippers to go with her white cut-velvet gown. She fell in love with a lord who lived in a castle.

The Astaires were a smash, and not just Adele. The newspaper said, "Fred, in particular, is wonderful with his footwork." More and more, the footwork was of Fred's own invention. Ideas came to him as he lay awake at four o'clock in the morning. He jumped from bed to try things out—and woke Adele with his humming and thumping.

Then one day in 1932, Adele told Fred she was going to marry her Lord Cavendish and stop dancing. She was thirty-four, and she didn't want to work so hard anymore. They had performed together for nearly thirty years, shared berths and boarding houses, lessons and sled rides, flops and hits, dressing rooms, and an egg cut in half. There had always been two Astaires, never one. She was his one true friend. What would Fred do without Adele?

He threw himself into work. He gathered everything he had done and seen in vaudeville and musical comedy, all the way back to when he was a boy watching the other acts from the wings, and he put bits from here and there into a new routine that was unlike anything he had ever done. *"Night and day, you are the one / Only you beneath the moon or under the sun,"* Fred sang in a nimble voice and glided with a new partner, Claire Luce, across the stage on a cushion of air.

Adele came to see the show. She sat in the audience and watched her brother perform for the first time. "He is wonderful," she said.

But Fred was growing tired of doing the same thing in the same show night after night. He was eager to try something new. Moving pictures were the big new thing. True, his face was no movie-star face, and there wasn't much of his kind of dancing in the movies—yet. He would have to work very, very hard.

Fred flew to Hollywood in 1933 and plunged into making movies. He got a kick out of inventing dances that were not confined to the stage but skipped up stairs or spun across a lagoon. He had a ball figuring out how to dance with a golf club in the movie *Carefree* and a coat rack in *Royal Wedding*. If something went wrong—as it did in *Top Hat* when his partner Ginger Rogers wore a dress made of feathers that flew off like hundreds of moths —they simply filmed the number again.

Fred didn't mind having to do a scene over and over ten times in little bits in front of the cameras. He liked being able to get the scene as close to perfect as he could make it. When it was done, captured on film forever, he was free to go on to something new—and even more difficult. Use a cane like a machine gun? Dance with firecrackers? What else? What fun!

The End

FURTHER READING

Fred Astaire's autobiography is *Steps in Time* (Cooper Square Press, 2000).

Fred Astaire: His Friends Talk, edited by Sarah Giles, is a collection of quotes from people who knew him, from movie stars to his maid (Doubleday, 1988).

There are several abundantly illustrated coffee-table books. The best, because it covers the vaudeville career as well as the movies, and is responsibly written, is *Fred Astaire,* by Benny Green (Exeter Books, 1979). *Starring Fred Astaire,* by Stanley Green and Burt Goldblatt (Dodd, Mead & Company, 1973), is useful for its many and rare photographs.

Another valuable illustrated book is *Astaire Dancing: The Musical Films,* by John Mueller (Knopf, 1985). It describes in fascinating detail every dance number in every movie via text and movie-frame enlargements—some 2,300 images in all.

The Fred Astaire & Ginger Rogers Book, by Arlene Croce, is a joyful critique of the Fred-and-Ginger films (Vintage Books, 1972).

Tap! The Greatest Tap Dance Stars and their Stories, 1900–1955, by Rusty E. Frank, demonstrates the variety of tap styles and thirty colorful characters who chose tap as their medium (Da Capo Press, 1994). Includes an interview with Fred's assistant, Hermes Pan.

Vaudeville U.S.A., by John E. DiMeglio, offers a fairly complete picture of the vaudeville era (Bowling Green University Popular Press, 1973).

LISTENING

There's a rare chance to hear Adele and Fred singing together on some cuts, including "The Whichness of the Whatness," in *Fred Astaire: The Complete London Sessions* (3 CDs; EMI 7243 5 20045 2 2).

On *The Astaire Story* (2 CDs; Polygram Records 835 649-2) Fred sings with a jazz combo that includes pianist Oscar Peterson and bassist Ray Brown. Fred said he "had a ball" making this album.

VIEWING

Some favorites among Fred's thirty movie musicals are *Top Hat, Follow the Fleet, Swing Time,* and *Carefree,* all with Ginger Rogers; *Easter Parade,* with Judy Garland; *Royal Wedding,* with Jane Powell; and *Funny Face,* with Audrey Hepburn (available on video and DVD).

Not on video or DVD but worth searching for in film libraries are the documentary *Fred Astaire: Puttin' on His Top Hat* (1980) and the TV specials he made late in his career. They include *An Evening with Fred Astaire* (1958), which earned him an Emmy Award for best actor, and *Astaire Time* (1960). On TV he danced with Barrie Chase, possibly his favorite—and best—partner.

ON THE WEB

A thorough—and thoroughly entertaining—website is www.AlsoDances.net.

For Nolan — R. O.

To Marie at the Studio — S. J.

Text copyright © 2007 by Roxane Orgill
Illustrations copyright © 2007 by Stéphane Jorisch

First edition 2007

Library of Congress Cataloging-in-Publication Data is available.

Library of Congress Catalog Card Number 2006040068

ISBN 978-0-7636-2121-6

2 4 6 8 10 9 7 5 3 1

Printed in China

This book was typeset in Optima.
The illustrations were done in ink, watercolor, and gouache, with digital support.

Candlewick Press
2067 Massachusetts Avenue
Cambridge, MA 02140

visit us at www.candlewick.com

ACKNOWLEDGMENTS
The author wishes to thank the following:

Ava Astaire McKenzie and her husband, Richard McKenzie, for sharing their memories and observations.

Special Collections at Boston University, for use of the invaluable Fred and Adele Astaire Collections,
including the scrapbooks their mother kept during their vaudeville and theater careers,
and letters written by Fred to his mother and sister.

The B & O Railroad Museum, the National Railroad Historical Society,
and the guys at www.railfan.net, for help in research on trains.

The New York Public Library's research divisions, specifically the
Humanities and Social Sciences Library and the Library for the Performing Arts.